P-51 MUSTANG

Jeffrey L. Ethell

Motorbooks International
Publishers & Wholesalers ®

First published in 1993 by Motorbooks International Publishers & Wholesalers, PO Box 2, 729 Prospect Avenue, Osceola, WI 54020 USA

Motorbooks International books are also available at discounts in bulk quantity for industrial or sales-promotional use. For details write to Special Sales Manager at the Publisher's address

Library of Congress Cataloging-in-Publication Data

Ethell, Jeffrey L.
    P–51 Mustang / Jeffrey L. Ethell.
        p.   cm. — (Enthusiast color series)
    Includes index.
    ISBN 0-87938-818-8
    1. Mustang (Fighter planes)   I. Title.
        II. Series.
  UG1242.F5E866   1994
  358.4'383—dc20   93-13062

On the front cover: Li'l Kitten was a veteran 357th Fighter Group P-51B flown by Lt. Louis Fechet with an improved-vision Malcolm hood made in England. This Mustang was originally delivered to the group unpainted, but the 357th was fond of camouflage, so they repainted it; a dead give-away is the masked off data block with the natural-metal background. Since the skin was unprimed on these newer aircraft, the paint often flaked off, giving the airplanes a well used look. *Robert Astrella*

On the frontispiece: John P. "Jeep" Crowder flying a 524th Squadron A-36A in 1943, over Mt. Etna, Sicily. With the addition of a bar to the national marking, then a red surround, the A-A unit and individual-aircraft codes had to be moved to the tail to make room. By this time about half of the Invader production run had been destroyed, with no replacement A-36s on line. As a result, the remaining aircraft were very tired and much in need of spare parts. They flew through the spring of 1944 until replaced by P-47s, and in some dire cases, P-40s. *John P. Crowder via Dorothy Helen Crowder*

On the title page: A 339th Fighter Group P-51D, *Arrow Head,* visits Mt. Farm, England, in late 1944 from its base at Fowlmere. *Robert Astrella*

On the back cover: The P-51K flown by John C. Casey of the 357th Fighter Group. *Arnold N. Delmonico*

Printed and bound in Hong Kong

Contents

Chapter 1 **World War II and the Postwar Years** 7

Chapter 2 **The Mustang in the Korean War** 71

Chapter 3 **Postwar Foreign Service** 91

Index 96

Chapter 1

World War II and the Postwar Years

Foaling of a Mustang

"Sired by the English out of an American mother," said Assistant US Air Attache in London, Maj. Thomas Hitchcock, in 1942. The North American P-51 Mustang, against steep odds, emerged at the end of World War II as the finest all-around piston-engine fighter in service.

During the first months of the war the British and French renewed their efforts to purchase US-built aircraft, settling on the P-40. Lt. Benjamin S. Kelsey, head of the Army Air Corps Pursuit Projects Office at Wright Field, and his boss, Col. Oliver P. Echols regretted this since it would push a new Curtiss fighter, the XP-46, off the assembly lines. Air Corps commander Gen. H. H. "Hap" Arnold decided he could not spare the four-month lag in production to change from the P-40 to the P-46—if America were drawn into the war, quantity would be drastically needed.

In January 1940, recalled Kelsey, "Echols made a suggestion to the Anglo-French Purchasing Commission to find a manufacturer who wasn't already bogged down in high-priority stuff. Curtiss-Wright and the Air Corps would make available all the data we had on the XP-46 to help them build a new fighter. This was our secret talk in the halls to get P-46s in place of the P-40, to find some way of getting around the problem."

Opposite page
P-51Cs of the 51st Fighter Group on the line at Kunming, China, 1945. Originally assigned to the Tenth Air Force with P-40s, the group was transferred to the Fourteenth Air Force in October 1943 to defend the eastern end of the route over the Hump. By the time the 51st was given Mustangs in 1945 the group was harassing Japanese shipping in the Red River delta and supporting Chinese ground troops in their drive along the Salween River. *US Air Force*

First filly in a long long line of thorough-breds—the NA-73X during an early test flight, most likely in the spring of 1941 after it was rebuilt following a crash landing on 20 November 1940. Though the Army Air Corps was not the direct buyer, the regulation red, white, and blue stripes have been painted on the rudder. *North American via Larry Davis*

Scouting for other companies to build the P-40, the commission was drawn to North American Aviation, which had done a sterling job in providing Harvard trainers. The company made it clear they had no desire to build another firm's fighter; they wanted to design one themselves.

Commission member Sir Henry Self approached North American president James H. "Dutch" Kindelberger about designing such a fighter. By April 1940 NAA Vice President J. Leland Atwood had negotiated an agreement. Donovan R. Berlin, designer of the P-40, had spent the better part of the past two years developing the XP-46. With his go-ahead, Atwood bought the data, along with the results of how the aborted belly radiator scoop worked on the original XP-40, for $56,000. On 4 May, North American signed a Foreign Release Agreement with the Air Corps permitting sale of the Model NA-73 overseas, providing that two examples were supplied to the Army. Kelsey and Echols had maneuvered hard to get their new fighter built at a time when the Air Corps had no procurement money.

North American's Chief Engineer Raymond Rice and his team, under Chief Designer Edgar Schmued, began a seven-day work week to produce the fighter. Wing designer Larry Waite incorporated, at the insistence of Edward Horkey (aerodynamicist), the NACA (National Advisory Committee for Aeronautics) laminar-flow wing section, which had not been in the original design concept. Kelsey had pushed behind the scenes with NACA's Eastman Jacobs to get the new wing design into the project, and soon Jacobs was with the North American team on the West Coast. "All this happened," recalled Kelsey, "without anybody at Wright Field

having the foggiest notion of what was going on. We had to stay out of it because it was a British procurement." The North American team's genius resulted in the best design possible around the radical NACA laminar-flow wing section.

Though the Curtiss data was shipped by crate to California, Atwood later said not much of it was used in the final design. Others inside the industry, particularly Don Berlin and others at Curtiss, said otherwise from the time the Mustang became famous.

The first production Mustang, AG345, high in the southern California skies. After the crash of the NA-73X, the lagging flight-test schedule was commenced with AG345, which was flown for the first time by Louis Wait on 23 April 1941. It was subsequently retained by North American Aviation (NAA) for project testing. *John Quincy via Stan Wyglendowski*

There was no 120-day requirement for completion of the prototype, as has often been asserted. The only completion date

A Mustang IA in RAF service. The basic difference between the Mustang I, which went operational in mid-1942, and the IA was armament. The Mustang I had four .50 caliber and four .30 caliber machine guns, while the IA had four 20mm cannon. The RAF and RCAF pilots flying these early Army Co-Operation Command Mustangs at low level knew they had a real winner, particularly in speed. Very few fighters could keep up with the early Allison powered Mustangs on the deck. *Robert Astrella*

noted in the contract was initial delivery by January 1941 and all 400 aircraft delivered by September 30, 1941. Using internal systems and components from the Harvard trainer such as hydraulics, wheels, brakes, and electrics, the men at North American pushed the NA-73X out of the shop in a remarkable 102 days, minus the engine, which arrived twenty days later. It was not until 26 October 1940 that Vance Breese took the prototype into the air from Mines Field, California, for the first time.

The ventral radiator scoop for oil and glycol cooling needed aerodynamic refinement. The problems it caused weren't

When the 631st Fighter-Bomber Squadron (Dive) was working up in the United States, its pilots flew a number of different fighters to gain experience. This A-36A Invader is carrying blue practice bombs at one of the small dirt strips the unit used in 1943. By the time the outfit was flying P-39s, it had been merged with the 630th Squadron to form the 514th Squadron of the 406th Fighter Group, which would convert to P-47s before going overseas. *John Quincy via Stan Wyglendowski*

Women Airforce Service Pilots (WASPs) Barbara Jane Erickson (left) and Evelyn Sharp (right) discuss flying the P-51A Mustang with Lt. Grover Bryon at Long Beach, California, June 1942. The WASPs did a tremendous job ferrying all types of Army aircraft, from PT-19s to B-29s, though they were never officially inducted into the service. Evelyn was later killed ferrying a P-38 Lightning. Barbara was awarded the Air Medal in 1943 for making four transcontinental flights in a little less than five days, ferrying a P-47, P-51, C-47 and P-38. *NASM*

solved until the scoop was redesigned and lowered away from the boundary-layer aerodynamic disturbances on the underside of the fuselage. The initial Mustangs, as a result, did not fully realize the benefit of the "Meredith effect" that resulted in the air exiting the scoop creating thrust, offsetting the drag caused by the scoop.

The first Mustang I, British production number AG345, was first flown on 23 April 1941. The Air Corps was to have received their first example, designated

This A-36A Invader dive-bomber was flown by John P. "Jeep" Crowder out of Gela, Sicily, with the 524th Squadron, 27th Fighter-Bomber Group. Conditions were marginal, to be kind, and often impossible, alternating between blowing dust and a sea of mud. Crowder had entered action with the 33rd Fighter Group by flying his P-40F off the carrier *Chenango* to French Morocco in late 1942 before transferring to the 27th to fly the dive-bomber version of the Mustang. *John P. Crowder via Dorothy Helen Crowder*

Following pages
Stateside maintenance on a P-51B, 1944. This working airplane has quite a few stains, including overflow from the fuel tank filler neck. The Mustang was a simple aircraft overall, as can be seen by the yellow and black flap down indicator markings—there was no flap indicator in the cockpit, other than the different detents,or notches, in the flap handle. *NASM*

XP-51, in February 1941 and the other in March, but the first airframe didn't arrive at Wright Field until August 24. The second came in December. Contrary to the long-standing story of official neglect delaying acceptance of the fighter by the newly redesignated Army Air Forces, delays were caused by numerous additional problems, not the least of which was chaos resulting from the bombing of Pearl Harbor eight days before the second XP-51 was delivered. According to a 1942 P-51 acceptance report, production delays, bad weather, gun charging system prob-

One of the first production P-51B-1s, long after its combat career had ended, serving time as a headquarters hack or operational training unit (OTU) machine in late 1944. By this time new P-51Ds were being supplied to fighter groups, though late production P-51Bs and Cs were still operational. The retrofitted Malcolm hood provided much improved pilot visibility and some pilots preferred these aircraft over the later bubble canopy D models. *Robert Astrella*

lems, needed refinements to the Allison engines, and the higher priorities given to other aircraft already being evaluated hampered the process.

On 7 July 1941, over a month before
the first XP-51 arrived at Wright Field,
the AAF placed an order for 150 P-51s to
be furnished to the RAF. Only 93 ended
up with the British. Fifty-five were kept
by the AAF, two being set aside for the
XP-78 project (later XP-51B) to fit a
Packard-built Rolls-Royce Merlin engine
to the airframe. This promising start was

55th Fighter Group buzz job, Wormingford,
England, 1945. This was by far the favorite
sport of fighter pilots in World War II,
regardless of the potential court martial after
it was over. There was something over-
powering about being young and in control
of a multi-thousand horsepower machine.
Robert T. Sand

As with these mechanics working on a 4th
Fighter Group P-51D at Debden, England,
mid 1944, most maintenance was done outside
during World War II, regardless of theater of
operations. Fortunately this is a mild English
summer. *US Air Force*

Another war-weary Mustang, this P-51B-5 was kept on strength with the 20th Fighter Group at Kings Cliffe in late 1944, early 1945, as a run-about and basic joy-rider. There was only so much life in these Mustangs and maintenance priority was always given to combat-capable aircraft. *Robert Astrella*

slowed by lack of funds, since no more money was available in that year's budget for fighter aircraft, but Echols, Kelsey, and Kindelberger found enough money in the attack portion of the AAF budget. The solution was, according to Kelsey, finding

the next number allocated for an aircraft, which happened to be A-36. Adding bomb racks and dive brakes to the airframe— and calling it an attack bomber instead of a fighter—kept the production line open. This risky move by a few maneuvering Army officers showed anything but neglect.

World War II

Before the first P-51 flew, an order was placed for 500 A-36 aircraft on April 16, 1942. By March 1943, when the first AAF Mustangs were ordered into combat in

The 336th Fighter Squadron's hack Mustang was a horse of a different color. The 4th Fighter Group had always been known for doing things with some dash but this two-seater had to be one of the more striking war-weary Mustangs in England, thanks to some dedicated mechanics. The aircraft, coded VF-4, is lined up at Debden with a 359th Fighter Group P-51D and several other Mustangs on 23 March 1945 during a meeting of fighter unit commanders to plan cover for the Rhine River crossing. *Edward B. Richie*

North Africa, the RAF's Army Co-Operation Command had been flying the fighter in combat for 10 months. Though British

Opposite page
Crew chief Johnny Ferra straps 4th Fighter
Group ace Don Gentile into *Shangri-La*, the
P-51B that Gentile rode to fame for two
months from February to April 1944. During a
low-level buzz job after the 13 April 1944
mission to Schweinfurt, Gentile misjudged
and flew into the ground, destroying his
legendary "kite." Group commander Don
Blakeslee had said that anyone pranging a
kite while stunting would be immediately
kicked out of the group. Blakeslee lived up to
his word and without even seeing Gentile,
booted him out and off to the States.
via Stan Piet

When Poland was overrun in 1939, many
Polish pilots were integrated into the RAF,
eventually forming squadrons and flying most
of the major British types. By mid-1944 these
squadrons were an active part of the RAF's
striking power. Some Polish units converted to
Mustang IIIs, then IVs, and flew them in
combat through the rest of the war on
long-range escort and deep fighter penetration.
As with most RAF Mustang IIIs, this No. 309
Squadron (Polish) aircraft has been retrofitted
with a Malcolm hood. Note the Polish insignia
on the lower front engine cowling. *John
Quincy via Stan Wyglendowski*

and American pilots found the Mustang to be faster than anything around at low level, it suffered greatly from lack of high altitude performance.

Waiting in the wings was a wizard for the Yank aircraft: just as Merlin was able to transform a young boy into King Arthur, so could the Rolls-Royce wizard of the same name transform a spirited American pony into a fiery thoroughbred.

After flying a Mustang I in April 1942, Rolls-Royce test pilot Ronald W. Harker went back to his company and asked if a Merlin 61 engine could be fitted to the excellent, low-drag Mustang airframe. Harker believed that the combination could result in the best fighter of the war, in spite of the British Air Ministry asking, "Why waste time on an untried, American-built aeroplane?" In spite of much opposition, five aircraft were set aside for modification.

Rolls-Royce let North American know what they were up to, so North American set aside two P-51 airframes to receive the American-built Packard Merlin. A friendly competition developed to see who would be the first to fly a Merlin Mustang. The

A 1st Air Commando Group P-51A flies close escort on former Flying Tiger R. T. Smith's B-25H over Burma. Under the talented leadership of Phil Cochran and Johnny Alison, the 1st became a guerrilla striking force that could hit targets with all manner of aircraft, from L-5s on up, in support of British Brigadier Orde Wingate's Chindits and the US Army's rough jungle war. *R.T. Smith*

A line of new P-51Cs in August 1944 at Dale Mabrey Field, Tallahassee, Florida, await their 3rd Air Commando Group pilots. The unit had just transitioned from P-40s before heading to the Philippines under the command of former Flying Tiger Arvid E. Olson, Jr. *Jacques Young*

British only just beat the Americans—Rolls-Royce flew their first conversion on 14 October 1942, and North American had the XP-51B up on November 30. The results were stunning, and almost exactly one year later the P-51B entered combat over Europe.

In spite of serious teething problems brought on by rushed development, the

The English winter of 1944–1945 was not kind, with the ground covered most of the time by frost or snow. *Rusty* was the P-51K assigned to Jeff French in the 339th Fighter Group at Fowlmere, England. When French finished his tour in January 1945, *Rusty* was reassigned to Bill Preddy, brother of leading Mustang ace George Preddy. Tragically both brothers were killed in action—George by American gunners who mistook his P-51 for a German fighter on Christmas Day 1944, and Bill by enemy fire on 17 April 1945 near Prague. The only difference between the K and D model Mustangs was the propeller: the K had one from the Aeroproducts factory, while the D had a Hamilton Standard with cuffs at the base of each blade.
L. Jeffrey French

25

When John C. Casey was assigned this P-51K at Leiston, he named it after his hometown. The red and yellow striped spinner and checkerboard cowl band were hallmarks of the 357th Fighter Group, one of the most aggressive Eighth Air Force fighter outfits.
Arnold N. Delmonico

Merlin Mustang could fly farther into enemy territory than any other fighter on the same amount of fuel, thus saving the AAF's strategic bombing campaign from annihilation at the hands of the Luftwaffe. By the end of World War II the P-51 reigned supreme on all fronts, its pilots having claimed more than 5,000 enemy aircraft destroyed, more than either the P-38 or the P-47.

The ground crew runs up "Lefty" Grove's 4th Fighter Group P-51D, VF-T, at Debden, England, in early 1945, just before a mission. The external tanks are hung and serviced and by the time Grove gets there the engine will be warm and ready for restart. *Francis M. Grove*

27

"Lefty" Grove's 336th Squadron P-51D sits on the line at Debden, England, in early 1945. Spawned from the RAF Eagle Squadrons, the 4th Fighter Group had a distinctive flavor in both its flying and its operational jargon: an airplane was a "kite," the intelligence scoop was the "gen," one didn't crash an airplane, he "pranged his kite." Grove was in front of a long line of replacement pilots who came directly from the United States Army Air Forces rather than through the RAF. *Francis M. Grove*

28

Mr. Ted belonged to 78th Fighter Group commander Frederic Gray, who was at the helm for almost two years, from May 1943 to February 1945. In that time the Duxford checker-nose gang traded in their P-47s for Mustangs and became one of the Eighth Air Force's premier fighter outfits. *Robert Astrella*

Following pages
An imposing view of a 357th Fighter Group Mustang. Since the clamshell fairing doors have not dropped down yet, the hydraulic system is still under pressure, indicating the aircraft has been run recently, and that the pilot or crew chief has not pulled the hydraulic pressure dump handle in the cockpit.
via Harry Friedman

A 4th Fighter Group P-51—*Nad* has been painted on the side in the distinctive style of Don Allen, the premier nose artist in the group, who was responsible for decorating some of the more famous aircraft in the ETO. *via Harry Friedman*

T he Seventh Air Force's P-51Ds had a single job, to escort B-29s on Very Long Range (VLR) missions into Japan and back, often up to ten hours at a time. Though the Mustang had a fine cockpit, it was a very uncomfortable place after a few hours.

This look across the 364th Fighter Group base at Honington, England, in late 1944 shows the life of the enlisted ground crew. On the right are unopened external fuel tank crates. In the background behind the two Mustangs are the gun butts for bore sighting the guns. And to the left is a line shack that was constructed from discarded fuel tank crates. Necessity drove men to find whatever comfort they could on these open fields, particularly in the winter, and the shacks became lifesavers. The bicycles were the standard mode of local transportation, unless one had enough rank to get a jeep. *Mark Brown/US Air Force Academy*

Marvin Arthur's *Blondie* was one of the finest of crew chief Don Allen's 4th Fighter Group nose art creations. Though named for Arthur's wife, the nose art came from Allen's imagination, as he recalled "sexy, but covered." *Donald E. Allen*

April 1945, Peretola, Italy. *Tempus Fugut* was the personal P-51D of 31st Fighter Group commander W. A. Daniel. The 31st was famous for flying Spitfires until almost mid-1944, when they transitioned to Mustangs. *Fred Bamberger*

A Chinese American Composite Wing (CACW) P-51D with the gear just about in the wells after takeoff at Nanking, China, in 1945. Within the CACW the 3rd and 5th Fighter Group flew P-40s, then Mustangs through the end of the war, primarily in close bomber-escort and ground attack missions. *George McKay via Larry Davis*

Kiangwan Airfield, Shanghai, 1945. On the line among the B-25s, C-47s, and C-46s are an F-6D Mustang of the 530th Squadron, 311th Fighter Group and a P-47D of the 93rd Squadron, 81st Fighter Group. *George McKay via Larry Davis*

Below
The 23rd Fighter Group was a direct descendant of Claire Chennault's American Volunteer Group, the Flying Tigers, flying P-40s, then P-51s through the end of the war. These 75th Squadron P-51Ds rest on the line in China with Thunderbolts at the end of the war. *George McKay via Larry Davis*

These P-51Ds at Mt. Farm, England, carry the simple 7th Photo Group markings of blue spinner and red cowl stripe, plus the red rudder normally painted on 13th Photo Squadron F-5 Lightnings. In January 1945 the 7th began to receive Mustangs to provide fighter escort for its F-5s, armed with nothing but cameras deep in enemy territory . . . a dangerous job. *Robert Astrella*

Below
The 7th Photo Group recorded 4,251 sorties and fifty-eight aircraft missing in action, among them five P-51s. The Mustangs flew 880 sorties, getting one probable and one damaged while protecting the Lightnings. This 7th P-51D sits at Mt. Farm with full external tanks and "putt-putt" auxiliary power unit on the left ready to plug in for start. The clamshell wheel fairing doors are not fully down, indicating the Mustang was run and warmed up a short time before by its crew chief. *Robert Astrella*

Above
Happy IV was flown by 339th Fighter Group commander William C. Clark. The eleven flags represented one air and ten ground kills while his wife's name, *Dotty*, was painted on the canopy frame. The dispersal area at Fowlmere, like so many other bases around the world, was covered by pierced steel plank (PSP) to prevent the aircraft from getting mired down in the mud. *James R. Starnes/Harry Corry via Robert S. DeGroat*

The 504th Fighter Squadron at dispersal, Fowlmere, summer 1945. The interlocked wooden plank on the ground was an alternative to PSP in keeping fighters free from the clutches of English mud. With the war over, the 339th Fighter Group, along with the rest of the Eighth Air Force, had very little flying to do. Everyone was waiting to go home. *James R. Starnes*

Jerry Collins in his *Lady of the Sky* over Japan in September 1945 with the 3rd Squadron, 3rd Air Commando Group. As the war ended, the Army Air Forces moved into Japan to become a part of the occupation forces with the 3rd going from Ie Shima to Atsugi on 20 September 1945. *Jacques Young*

Left
Triple Threat was a 3rd Squadron, 3rd Air Commando Group P-51D at Chitose, Japan, after the war. The group had many different colored spinners, particularly blue, red, and yellow, but the color on the tail denoted the squadron—blue for the 3rd and red for the 4th. *Paul Vercammen via David W. Menard*

Previous page
R. Vern Blizzard with *Punkie II*, 5Q-O, his 504th Squadron, 339th Fighter Group P-51D, at Fowlmere, England, 1945. Blizzard put his wife's nickname on the Mustang for good luck and apparently it worked since he made it through to the end of the war. *Robert V. Blizzard*

Another 3rd Air Commando Mustang, *Gypsy* had a good representation of Milton Caniff's Miss Lace as nose art. Caniff's creations were extremely popular during World War II, particularly his women, including the Dragon Lady and Burma. *Paul Vercammen via David W. Menard*

Though this shot was posed by the AAF photographer, these 4th Fighter Group armorers at Debden, England give a pretty good idea of the wallop packed by the six .50 caliber machine guns and ammunition that went into a P-51D. *NASM*

By the time World War II was over AAF units were faced with a surplus of aircraft and nowhere to go. These 55th Fighter Group Mustangs sit idle at Wormingford, England, in June 1945 awaiting an inspection. Eventually the '51s were scrapped. *Robert T. Sand*

Left
A late-model P-51D, with a new paddle-blade Hamilton Standard propeller, on the line at Ontario Army Air Base, California, 1945. Ontario was home to a number of AAF training units, flying everything from Stearmans to P-38s to captured enemy aircraft like the Japanese Zero. Most of Southern California was a mass of military training fields during the war, ripe with the opportunity for pilots to bounce each other unannounced. *Norman W. Jackson*

Several Mustangs of the 46th Squadron, 21st Fighter Group sit on the volcanic ash of Iwo Jima in 1945. The Seventh Air Force's P-51Ds had a single job, to escort B-29s on Very Long Range (VLR) missions into Japan and back, often up to ten hours at a time. Though the Mustang had a fine cockpit, it was a very uncomfortable place after a few hours.
Russ Stauffer via John & Donna Campbell

Below
The cinders and blowing volcanic dust on Iwo Jima took quite a toll on engines and moving parts. The black ash these 72nd Squadron, 21st Fighter Group Mustangs sit on at Iwo was like nothing anyone had ever seen.
Russ Stauffer via John & Donna Campbell

The flagship, #200, of the 21st Fighter Group, carrying the tail stripe colors of all three squadrons, lands at Tinian in 1945. The group was based at Iwo Jima to provide VLR escort missions for the B-29s of the Twentieth Air Force. *Russ Stauffer via John & Donna Campbell*

New Mustangs at Leyte, October 1945, with nowhere to go and nothing to do. In spite of the war's end, the incredible flow of materiel to the Pacific was hard to shut off, which resulted in new airplanes with no combat time being junked. *D. Watt via David W. Menard*

When the 475th Fighter Group let go of its P-38s after the war, the unit was transitioned into Mustangs, which quickly got painted up in their Satan's Angels markings. This 431st Squadron P-51D in Japan, 1946, reflects the change. *US Air Force Museum*

Below

In Germany, without a war on, flying time was cut to the bone and once-fierce Mustangs were put out to pasture. With the markings scrubbed off and her paint peeling, it's hard to tell if this P-51D belonged to the 363rd Fighter Group or the 354th Fighter Group—both had yellow nose markings like this. It really didn't matter. *Tootsie* was broken apart, burned, and left where she sat in Germany. *Fagen via David W. Menard*

Even in the very late 1940s wartime
Mustangs could be seen rotting away, clearly
evident here at the University of Illinois
Airport in 1949. These were stateside training
P-51Cs acquired for the local tech school.
C. Grahan via David W. Menard

Right
Postwar air racing was dominated by
Mustangs, particularly the Thompson and
Bendix races which centered around
Cleveland. The greatest winner of them all
was Hollywood stunt pilot Paul Mantz who
won the Bendix three years in a row with his
P-51Cs, among them the great No. 60 seen
here just after landing. The oil and exhaust
trails tell the story of this cross-country race
from California—push the power as far as the
engine could stand and don't back it off until
landing. *via Walter E. Ohlrich, Jr.*

With surplus P-51s available all day long for $1,500, there was quite a field for each of the post-war races, painted in all kinds of garish schemes.

One of the most radically modified of the racing Mustangs was the stunning, dark green *Beguine*, which was entered in the 1949 Thompson. The belly scoop radiators were removed and installed in the wingtips in hopes of reducing drag. Though there was great anticipation over how the ex-fighter would do, pilot Bill Odom crashed into a house on the course after cutting a pylon, killing himself, a mother and her child. Unlimited air racing was over until 1964 with the advent of less populated courses and a dimming public memory of the crash's innocent victims. *via Walter W. Ohlrich, Jr.*

The name *City of Lynchburg* was carried on all of Woody Edmundson's racing Mustangs, including No. 15 here at Cleveland for the 1947 Thompson Trophy race. With surplus P-51s available all day long for $1,500, there was quite a field for each of the post-war races, painted in all kinds of garish schemes. This sunburst pattern was typical of most airshow aircraft during the period. *Ole C. Griffith*

As bombing distances grew ever longer during World War II, planners called for fighters that could stay with the bombers on extended-range missions. North American offered what was, basically, two lightweight P-51Fs attached, carrying two pilots, with P-51H outer wing panels and engines—the XP-82 Twin Mustang, which flew for the first time on 16 June 1945. This is the first P-82E. *Ron Picciani*

Betty Jo, a P-82B, taxies in at New York in 1947 after setting a record by flying 5,000 miles from Hawaii nonstop. In addition to the four underwing external fuel tanks, more tanks were added behind each pilot. It was an epic flight, giving the new US Air Force much-needed publicity for its long-range bomber-escort program during the postwar cutbacks. *NASM*

A line of 27th Fighter-Escort Group P-82Es at Howard AFB, Panama. The "Double-Breasted Mustangs" in the foreground were attached to the 524th Squadron. The first Twin Mustangs were delivered to the 27th in March 1948 to escort the newly created Strategic Air Command's B-29s, B-50s, and B-36s until the summer of 1950 when the redesignated 27th Wing began to receive F-84E Thunderjets. *Ray Williams/Warren Thompson via Don Spry*

The postwar growth of the US Air Force, born out of the wartime US Army Air Forces in 1947, centered around SAC's long-range-bomber capability. This gave urgent life to the F-82E. These 27th Fighter-Escort Group Twin Mustangs have just left Bergstrom Air Force Base, Texas, on a long-range-escort mission carrying extensive external fuel. *B. Mitchell via David W. Menard*

The 52nd All Weather Group at Mitchel Field, Long Island, flew colorful F-82F all-weather interceptors (the new term for night fighters) with radar pods mounted under the center wing. The right cockpit was reconfigured for a radar operator, while the pilot handled the flying from the left. *Ron Picciani*

Post-war decision making on a standard
fighter for Reserve and Air National Guard
units led to the P-51 being kept while other
leftover piston fighters were given to other
countries or scrapped. There were brand-new
P-51Ds at every turn so it didn't take long to
spread them out to many different squadrons
across the country. Mustangs would stay in
service with the Guard until 1957.
W. J. Balogh via David W. Menard

Air National Guard units came up with imaginative schemes for their F-51Ds but none more so than the Kentucky boys' target sleeve tug, done up in bright yellow, at the ANG gunnery meet at Boise, Idaho, in October 1954. *P. Paulsen via David W. Menard*

The West Virginia Air National Guard was the last ANG unit to fly the F-51D. The Coonskin Boys' colorful postwar period is well reflected by these two Mustangs over the Mountain State. The extended blue nose was inspired by WVANG pilot Edwin L. Heller who originally flew with the 352nd Fighter Group in World War II, the "Blue Nosed Bastards of Bodney." The 167th Fighter Squadron's rampant unicorn jumping past a lightning bolt was the insignia of the old wartime 369th Squadron, 359th Fighter Group, which had been reassigned to the West Virginia unit. Both combat traditions were carried over with much pride. *Ken Hoylman via David W. Menard*

During 1949 inauguration ceremonies for President Harry Truman, WVANG F-51Ds flew escort for B-29s and B-36s as they passed over the ceremony, the last mass piston fly-over of any size for the nation's capital. A short time later the colorful World War II-inspired markings would disappear and an era came to an end. *Ken Hoylman via David W. Menard*

Below
Maj. John B. England taxies out at Nellis Air Force Base, Nevada, 1950, in the lead Mustang of the Red Devils aerobatic team, a forerunner of the jet teams to come. England, who was credited with 17.5 kills with the 357th Fighter Group in World War II, was as colorful as the water-based paint on his F-51, which was painted a solid red. The three wingmen were painted partially red. The paint didn't last long but it could easily be reapplied for the next show. *G. Gravenstine via David W. Menard*

An F-51D of the Minnesota ANG runs up in the winter cold with long-range, jet-style external fuel tanks typical of 1950s-era Mustangs in military service. Though the Guard used both the F-51 and F-47, the Thunderbolt disappeared almost overnight while the Mustang survived to make its way into the civil inventory. Pilots going to Korea would soon regret the Jug's demise. *via Dick Phillips*

Those Mustangs that were kept in the regular Air Force had their share of colorful markings as well. This F-51D at Luke Air Force Base, Arizona, carries the yellow and black checkerboards of the Fighter Weapons School, a tradition carried on to the present day. By the end of the Korean War the last Mustang had been retired from the US Air Force with only the Guard to carry on. *David W. Menard Collection*

The Kentucky ANG lined up at Boise, Idaho, 1954, during annual gunnery training revealed quite a variety in colors and markings, down to the yellow target-sleeve tug at the end. *P. Paulsen via David W. Menard*

As the F-51H was phased out of the active US Air Force inventory into the Guard, pilots were impressed with its hot-rod performance. The only production lightweight Mustang, it served escort-fighter duty with SAC, but there were never enough built to provide spares for an extended service life. The Maryland ANG flew them extensively, at one time putting up a four-ship aerobatic team known as the Guardian Angels. *Ron Picciani*

For several years Grumman Aircraft Corporation flew an F-51H as a chase plane for its new jet fighters. The excellent acceleration and top speed of the last Mustang gave Grumman pilots quite a credible chase capability until lack of spares and overhaul facilities made them put the worn-out warhorse to pasture. *H.G. Martin via David W. Menard*

Chapter 2

The Mustang in the Korean War

When the Korean War broke out, the Mustang was thrown straight back into action as the F-51,along with its bigger brother, the F-82 Twin Mustang. The US Air Force had been born in 1947 and the next year P for Pursuit changed to F for Fighter in the Air Force aircraft-designation system. When North Korean Yak fighters strafed Kimpo Airfield on 27 June 1950, F-82s shot down three of them to make the first kills of the war. Though taking a prop driven fighter into a jet war seemed like going backwards, the Mustangs could loiter over ground targets for an hour while the jets could only stay fifteen minutes if they were lucky. The F-51 and F-82 could also use shorter runways, which were usually closer to the front lines.

Unfortunately, the Mustang's liquid cooling system was very vulnerable to damage from ground fire, and many Mustang pilots were killed or became POWs who would not have gone down had they been flying an air-cooled fighter. Though not assigned to the air-to-air combat role, F-51 pilots did tangle with Yaks, shooting down at least four, and the MiG-15, though none of the jets were shot down. Still this wonderful fighter of a bygone era was an antique in the jet age.

Pilots not used to the torque problems in a high-powered piston fighter tended to wreck them regularly, particularly if they had been accustomed to flying with their

Opposite page
No.2 Squadron, South African Air Force, F-51Ds marshall for takeoff on a strike out of Chinhae during the Korean War. They carry the standard close-air-support armament of 500 pound bombs, two five-inch rockets under each wing and full ammunition. A number of Mustang units flew from Chinhae, making logistical support a bit simpler—though nothing was simple in this so-called "limited war." *US Air Force*

This F-82G, *Bucket of Bolts*, made the first kill of the Korean War while attached to the 68th Fighter (All Weather) Squadron. On 27 June 1950 Lts. William Hudson and Carl Fraser downed a Yak-7U in the morning during an attack on Kimpo Airfield by five enemy aircraft. Before the day was over another two aircraft were shot down by Twin Mustangs. *Boardman C. Reed via Don Spry*

feet on the floor. From January 1950 to January 1952 there were 462 major Mustang accidents, over half due to pilot error. Combat losses were even heavier and the Air Force had to pour a continual stream of replacement aircraft and pilots into the fighter-bomber units. By mid-war, all the Mustangs were withdrawn after fighting the very contest most pilots knew to be the most dangerous in World War II: at

low level, antiaircraft fire always had, and always would, take more lives than enemy fighters.

Another view of *Bucket of Bolts,* the Twin Mustang that made the first kill of the Korean War on 27 June 1950. Here she rests at K-2, Taegu, on 16 June 1951 after a year in combat. Twin Mustangs were used primarily for ground support, though night fighting capability was retained to deal with nuisance raids from Bed Check Charlies which droned over to rob people of sleep. *Boardman C. Reed via Dave McLaren*

A 40th Squadron, 35th Fighter Group F-51D has just pulled to a stop on the ramp in Japan, 1950, as the ground crewman moves to chock the wheels. The 35th's squadrons formed the basis for the initial cadre of pilots to take the Mustang back into combat when the Korean War broke out. *Ray Stewart/Warren Thompson via Tom Foote*

Below
The 40th Fighter Squadron line at Johnson Field, Japan, early 1950. The pre-World War II-style rudder stripes were a part of the 35th Fighter Group's colors before the Korean War broke out but they would soon disappear as Mustangs were pressed back into the close-air-support role, one for which it was ill suited due to the vulnerability of its liquid cooling system. *Paul Wilkins via Tom Foote*

Maj. William O'Donnell, commander of the 36th Fighter-Bomber Squadron, runs up *Mac's Revenge*, named for his niece. The other side of the airplane was labled by the crew chief as *O'l Anchor Ass*. The 8th Fighter Group had been flying F-80C Shooting Stars, but with the beginning of the Korean War the jets were taken away and replaced by the Mustangs the pilots had thought were well behind them. The 36th Squadron insignia leers from beneath the name. *William J. O'Donnell*

As a radio change is made on Bill O'Donnell's 36th Squadron F-51D at Tsuiki, Japanese personnel are busy polishing the skin of the aircraft to a bright mirror finish. The Japanese were known for their skill at making Mustangs shine by using quantities of fuller's earth as a very fine, almost talcum powder consistency, abrasive. The results drew a consistent business for the Japanese who were happy for the extra wages. *William J. O'Donnell*

Napalm-loading operations on the 36th Fighter-Bomber Squadron line at Tsuiki. Japanese girls are rolling fuel barrels across the ramp so the jellied gasoline mixture can be loaded into the drop tanks. For such a simple procedure, the results were frightening on the other end. *William J. O'Donnell*

Robert "Pancho" Pasqualicchio with his 67th Fighter-Bomber Squadron F-51D, *OL' NaDSoB*, at Chinhae, Korea, in 1951. Other 18th Fighter-Bomber Group Mustangs, painted with sharkmouths, can be spotted in the background. The 18th did a sterling job of ground support under an aggressive commander. Though the Mustang was a hold-over from a previous war, air-to-ground delivery techniques had not changed and the prop driven aircraft actually had better accuracy than the jets. Unfortunately the loss rates were horrendous. "I'd have bought my own P-47 at that point!" recalled Pasqualicchio. *Pancho Pasqualicchio*

Col. William "Willy" P. McBride, 18th Fighter-Bomber Group commander, got shot up during a ground-attack mission and had to make a forced landing at K-16, Yongdungpo, in May 1951. The fire crews did an outstanding job of making sure there would be no fire. *Pancho Pasqualicchio*

Chinhae, spring 1951: the unforgiving results of inexperience in high-performance piston fighters. A No. 2 Squadron, South African Air Force, ex-Sunderland flying boat pilot came to Korea with eight to ten hours in Spitfires, made a single familiarization flight in an F-51, then launched on his first combat mission fully loaded with bombs and rockets. He failed to hold the torque on takeoff, pulled to the left, and went into a group of twenty parked reserve-pool Mustangs. The pilot was killed instantly and several F-51s were lost. *Pancho Pasqualicchio*

Col. Rog Mercer in his 187th Fighter
Squadron, ANG, Mustang over the United
States. Many Air National Guard units flying
the F-51 were recalled to Korea, along with
pilots who had piston experience, to fill out the
Mustang groups going to combat. *Pancho
Pasqualicchio*

Right
Kimpo Airfield, South Korea, 1951: the
name on this 45th Tactical Reconnaissance
Squadron RF-51D, *Tulie, Scotty & ?*, referred
to the pilot's kids and pregnant wife. The 45th
had the very dangerous job of photographing
North Korean positions, convoys, and
movements up close with the rear-fuselage-
mounted cameras. Though bombs and rockets
could be carried, and often were, the
squadron's real value lay in providing close to
real-time intelligence for immediate strikes.
In World War II, the tac recce version of the
Mustang was known as the F-6. *Ron Picciani*

The first South Korean pilots to strike back after the North Korean invasion belonged to the Republic of Korea Air Force (ROKAF) 1st Fighter Squadron , flying F-51Ds with US Air Force leadership. The unit, initially trained under the command of Maj. Dean Hess in 1950, grew into an entire wing of Mustangs. This is the ROKAF line at Kangnung late in the war. *Alan Grindberg*

A ROKAF Mustang taxies in from a mission against North Korean positions. South Korean pilots who had wartime experience flying with the Japanese came up to speed in the F-51D relatively fast, whereas other newly trained pilots were almost overwhelmed with the demands of combat until getting enough time with their American advisors. *Ron Picciani*

An 8th Fighter-Bomber Group F-51D just after shutdown at K-2, Taegu, 2 July 1951. The ground crew has chocked the Mustang and is standing by to help the pilot unstrap. Flying the Mustang in Korea was rough, dirty work with very little reward. The jet units, particularly those flying F-86s over MiG Alley, got most of the glory while the majority of the war was an air-to-ground campaign. *Boardman C. Reed via Dave McLaren*

Jeannie, a 67th Fighter-Bomber Squadron F-51D, gets some much-needed maintenance at Chinhae. Conditions that World War II crews thought they'd never see again reappeared on the rugged, cold airfields of Korea where maintenance took place outside, and mechanics fought frost bite to work on their "antiques" from another war. *US Air Force*

Below
A 39th Squadron, 18th Fighter-Bomber Group F-51D has just taxied in at Chinhae, summer 1951, after a sortie. All of the underwing stores are gone and the residue from the .50 caliber machine guns has spread back across the wing. Mustangs in Korea were worked hard, taking heavy losses. *US Air Force*

RF-51Ds of the 45th Tactical Reconnaissance Squadron taxi out for a mission. Tac recce aircraft relied more on cameras than bombs and rockets. The idea was to loiter in enemy territory, photographing enemy positions and movements, strafing if necessary. The roaming fighters brought back a continual flow of pinpointed targets for concentrated strikes. *US Air Force*

Laborers load a No. 77 Squadron, Royal Australian Air Force F-51D with napalm at the 35th Fighter Group's Korean base. The jellied gasoline was pumped into large drop tanks already hung on the bomb racks; then an ignitor fuse was screwed in just before takeoff. *Gerald Brown*

Chapter 3

Postwar Foreign Service

By the end of the Korean War the Mustang had seen its last days fighting for the United States. Quite a number of F-51s were given to the Reserves and Air National Guard, where they served until 1957, but the majority went overseas under the Military Assistance Plan. An impressive list of foreign air forces were equipped with Mustangs, beginning with those allies that got the fighter in World War II: England, France, Australia, China, South Africa, Russia, South Korea, Taiwan, Philippines, Indonesia, Sweden, Switzerland, Italy, New Zealand, Israel, Canada, Haiti, Uruguay, Guatemala, Nicaragua, Costa Rica, Bolivia, Cuba, Venezuela, and the Dominican Republic.

Not until 1983 were the last active military Mustangs retired from service when the Dominican Republic traded them in for jets. The Mustang had been on continuous active duty forty-three years. From neglected foal to temperamental thoroughbred to charging warhorse, North American Aviation's P-51 Mustang became one of the greatest fighters of all time.

Opposite page
The Dominican Republic was one of the major foreign users of the Mustang, buying most of Sweden's postwar inventory (forty-two aircraft), then from several other air forces, and finally rebuilt from the Cavalier Aircraft Corporation under the Military Assistance Program. This photo shows the alert line at Santiago, Dominican Republic, the forward operating base closest to Cuba, May 1982. At this point in their career the Fuerza Aerea Dominicana (FAD) had used the Mustang as their primary fighter for thirty years, the longest continuous military use of the fighter on record. *Author*

As the Mustang was phased out of first-line
US Air Force service, many foreign air forces
continued to fly them. These Royal Canadian
Air Force Mustangs have just been sold
surplus after a long and happy career with
pilots who were fiercely proud of their mounts.
Ron Picciani

January 1963: this P-51D is still in first-line service with Guatemala, but the shiny T-33s in the background are a good indication of what is taking place. Soon all the Mustangs would be gone and the jet age would fully arrive in this small Central American country. *Robb Satterfield*

The Philippine Air Force used the F-51 as a primary fighter into the mid-1950s with the 6th, 7th and 8th Squadrons, 5th Fighter Wing. The wing commander's Mustang sits on the line at Nichols Field, 20 July 1958, with an 8th Squadron aircraft next to it. By 1959 the last P-51s were gone, replaced by F-86 Sabres. *Merle Olmsted*

Index

1st Air Commando Group, 23
1st Fighter Squadron (ROKAF), 84, 85
3rd Air Commando Group, 24, 40, 42
3rd Fighter Group, 36
4th Fighter Group, 15, 19, 28, 31, 40, 43
5th Fighter Group, 36, 95
6th Fighter Squadron, 95
7th Air Force, 68
7th Photo Group, 38
7th Squadron, 95
8th Fighter Group, 86
8th Fighter Squadron, 95
18th Fighter-Bomber Group, 78, 79, 87
20th Fighter Group, 18
21st Fighter Group, 45, 46
23rd Fighter Group, 37
27th Fighter-Bomber Group, 13
27th Fighter-Escort Group, 55, 56
33rd Fighter Group, 13
35th Fighter Group, 74, 89
36th Fighter-Bomber Squadron, 75, 76, 77
40th Fighter Squadron, 74
45th Tactical Reconnaissance Squadron, 88
51st Fighter Group, 7
52nd All Weather Group, 57
55th Fighter Group, 17
67th Fighter-Bomber Squadron, 78, 87
68th Fighter (All Weather) Squadron, 72
72nd Fighter Squadron, 45
75th Fighter Squadron, 37
77th Fighter Squadron, 89
81st Fighter Group, 37
93rd Squadron, 37
167th Fighter Squadron, 61
187th Fighter Squadron, 82
336th Fighter Squadron, 19, 28
339th Fighter Group, 39, 42
352nd Fighter Group, 61
354th Fighter Group, 47
357th Fighter Group, 26, 29, 62
359th Fighter Group, 18, 61
363rd Fighter Group, 47
364th Fighter Group, 33
369th Fighter Squadron, 61
406th Fighter Group, 11

475th Fighter Group, 47
504th Fighter Squadron, 39, 42
514th Squadron, 11
524th Squadron, 13, 55
530th Squadron, 37
631st Fighter-Bomber Squadron (Dive), 11

A-36A, 11, 19
Alison, Johnny, 23
Allen, Don, 34
Arnold, George Preddy, 7, 25
Arthur, Marvin, 34
Atwood, J. Leland, 8

Beguine, 50
Berlin, Don, 8, 9
Betty Jo, 54
Blakeslee, Don, 21
Blizzard, R. Vern, 42
Blondie, 34
Breese, Vance, 10
Bryon, Lt. Grover, 12
Bucket of Bolts, 72, 73

Casey, John C., 26
City of Lynchburg, 52
Clark, William C., 39
Cochran, Phil, 23
Collins, Jerry, 40
Crowder, John P., 13

Daniel, W. A., 35
Dotty, 39

Echols, Col. Oliver P., 7, 8, 18, 46
Edmundson, Woody, 52
Erickson, Barbara Jane, 12

Ferra, Johnny, 21
Fraser, Carl, 72
French, Jeff, 25

Gentile, Don, 21
Gray, Frederic, 29
Grove, "Lefty," 27, 28
Gypsy, 42

Happy IV, 39
Harker, Ronald W., 23
Heller, Edwin L., 61
Hess, Maj. Dean, 84

Hitchcock, Maj. Thomas, 7
Horkey, Edward, 8
Hudson, William, 72

Jacobs, 8
Jeannie, 87

Kelsey, Lt. Benjamin S., 7, 8, 18, 46
Kentucky ANG, 67
Kindelberger, James H., 8, 18, 46

Lady of the Sky, 40

Mac's Revenge, 75
Mante, Paul, 48
Maryland ANG, 68
McBride, Col. William P., 79
Mercer, Col. Rog., 82
Minnesota ANG, 63
Mr. Ted, 29

Nad, 31
No. 2 Squadron, 71
North American Aviation, 8, 9

O'Donnell, Maj. William, 75, 77
O'l Anchor Ass, 75
Odom, Bill, 50
OL' NaDSoB, 78
Olson, Arvid E., 24

P-40, 7, 8
P-46, 7
Pasqualicchio, Robert, 78
Preddy, Bill, 25
Punkie II, 42

Republic of Korea Air Force, 84, 85
Rice, Raymond, 8
Rusty, 25

Schmued, Edgar, 8
Self, Sir Henry, 8
Sharp, Evelyn, 12
Smith, R.T., 23

Tempus Fugut, 35
Tootsie, 47
Tulie, Scotty & ?, 82

Waite, Larry, 8
Waite, Louis, 9
Wingate, Brigadier Orde, 23